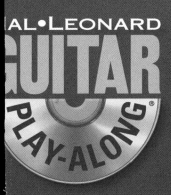

HAL•LEONARD

GUITAR
PLAY-ALONG®

VOL. 91

BLUES
INSTRUMENTALS

ISBN 978-1-4234-5342-0

HAL•LEONARD®
CORPORATION
7777 W. BLUEMOUND RD. P.O. BOX 13819 MILWAUKEE, WI 53213

Visit Hal Leonard Online at
www.halleonard.com

CONTENTS

GUITAR NOTATION LEGEND

THE MUSICAL STAFF shows pitches and rhythms and is divided by bar lines into measures. Pitches are named after the first seven letters of the alphabet.

TABLATURE graphically represents the guitar fingerboard. Each horizontal line represents a string, and each number represents a fret.

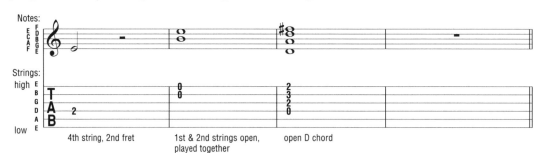

4th string, 2nd fret

1st & 2nd strings open, played together

open D chord

HALF-STEP BEND: Strike the note and bend up 1/2 step.

WHOLE-STEP BEND: Strike the note and bend up one step.

GRACE NOTE BEND: Strike the note and immediately bend up as indicated.

SLIGHT (MICROTONE) BEND: Strike the note and bend up 1/4 step.

BEND AND RELEASE: Strike the note and bend up as indicated, then release back to the original note. Only the first note is struck.

PRE-BEND: Bend the note as indicated, then strike it.

VIBRATO: The string is vibrated by rapidly bending and releasing the note with the fretting hand.

PALM MUTING: The note is partially muted by the pick hand lightly touching the string(s) just before the bridge.

HAMMER-ON: Strike the first (lower) note with one finger, then sound the higher note (on the same string) with another finger by fretting it without picking.

PULL-OFF: Place both fingers on the notes to be sounded. Strike the first note and without picking, pull the finger off to sound the second (lower) note.

LEGATO SLIDE: Strike the first note and then slide the same fret-hand finger up or down to the second note. The second note is not struck.

SHIFT SLIDE: Same as legato slide, except the second note is struck.

TRILL: Very rapidly alternate between the notes indicated by continuously hammering on and pulling off.

TAPPING: Hammer ("tap") the fret indicated with the pick-hand index or middle finger and pull off to the note fretted by the fret hand.

NATURAL HARMONIC: Strike the note while the fret-hand lightly touches the string directly over the fret indicated.

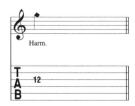

PINCH HARMONIC: The note is fretted normally and a harmonic is produced by adding the edge of the thumb or the tip of the index finger of the pick hand to the normal pick attack.

TREMOLO PICKING: The note is picked as rapidly and continuously as possible.

VIBRATO BAR DIVE AND RETURN: The pitch of the note or chord is dropped a specified number of steps (in rhythm), then returned to the original pitch.

VIBRATO BAR SCOOP: Depress the bar just before striking the note, then quickly release the bar.

VIBRATO BAR DIP: Strike the note and then immediately drop a specified number of steps, then release back to the original pitch.

Additional Musical Definitions

(accent) • Accentuate note (play it louder).

(staccato) • Play the note short.

D.S. al Coda • Go back to the sign (𝄋), then play until the measure marked "***To Coda***," then skip to the section labelled "**Coda**."

D.C. al Fine • Go back to the beginning of the song and play until the measure marked "***Fine***" (end).

Fill • Label used to identify a brief melodic figure which is to be inserted into the arrangement.

N.C. • Harmony is implied.

• Repeat measures between signs.

• When a repeated section has different endings, play the first ending only the first time and the second ending only the second time.

Blue Guitar

By Earl Hooker

Slow Blues ♩. = 70

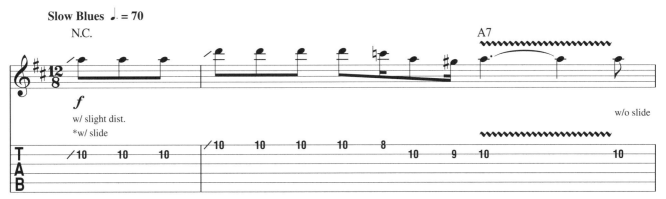

w/ slight dist.
*w/ slide

w/o slide

*Slide is worn on pinky throughout.

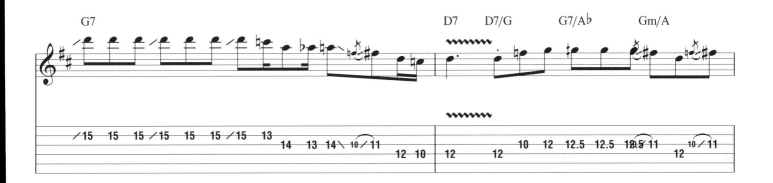

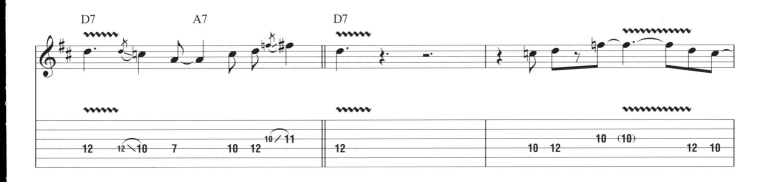

w/o slide

w/ slide

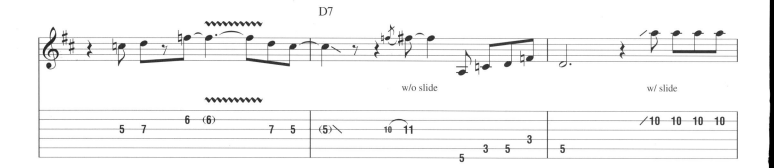

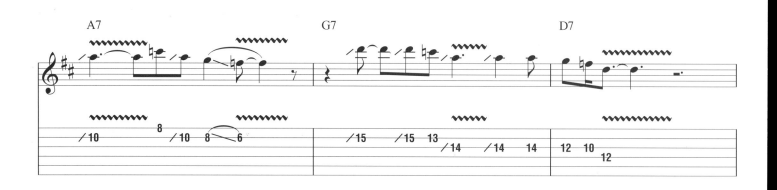

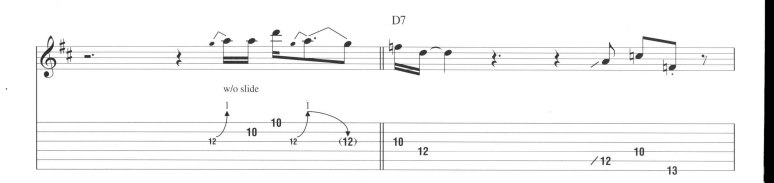

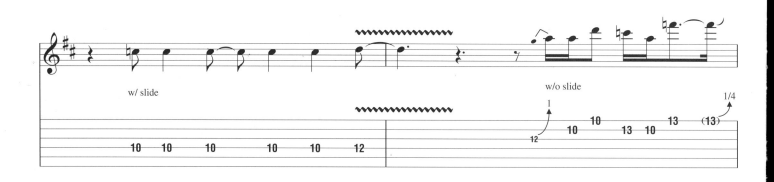

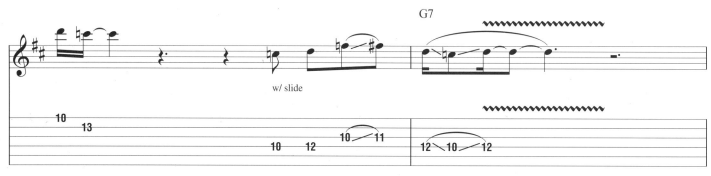

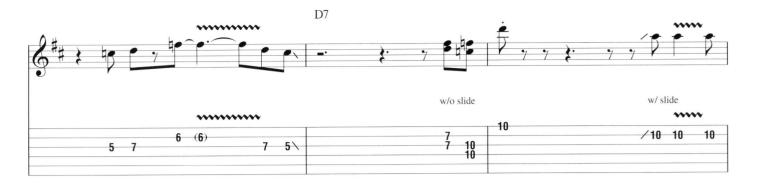

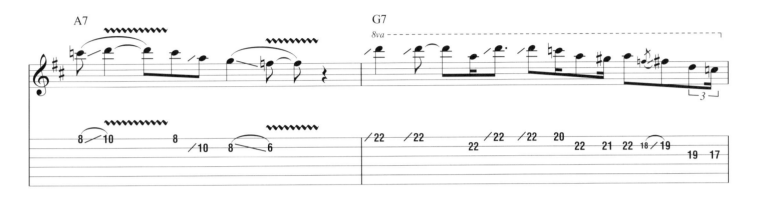

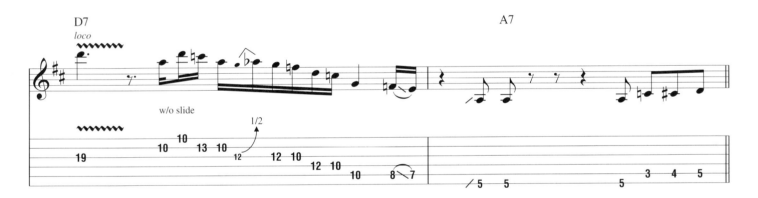

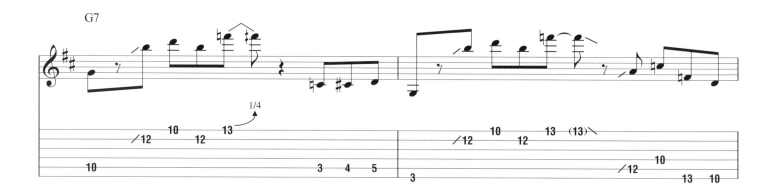

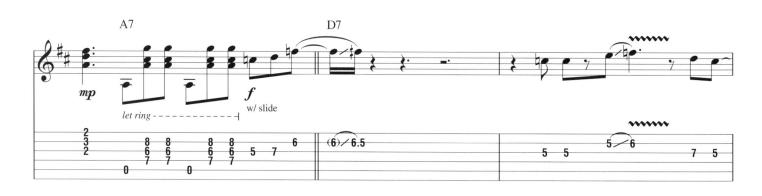

Begin fade

Fade out

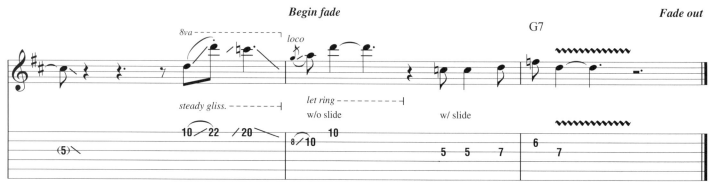

Just Like a Woman

By B.B. King

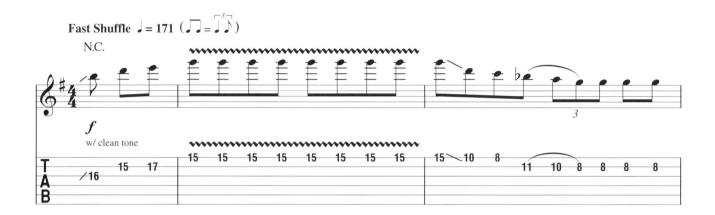

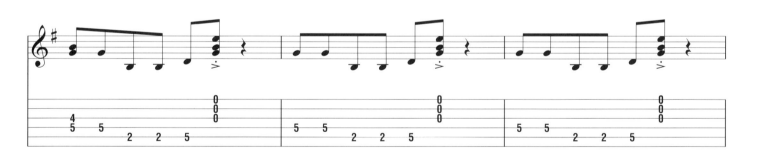

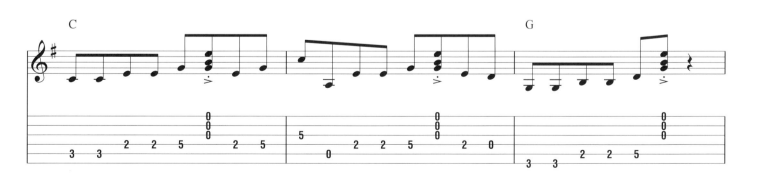

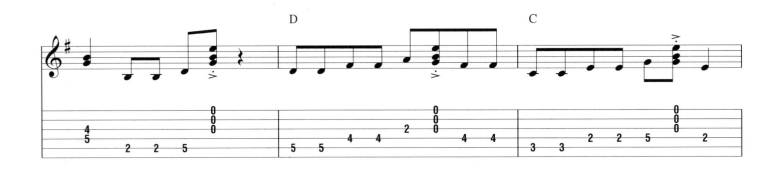

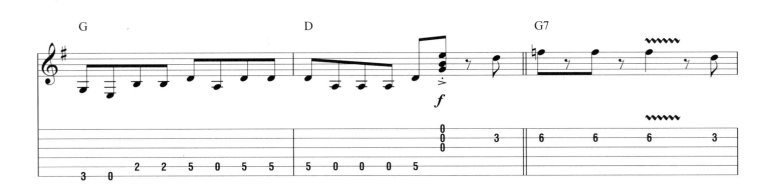

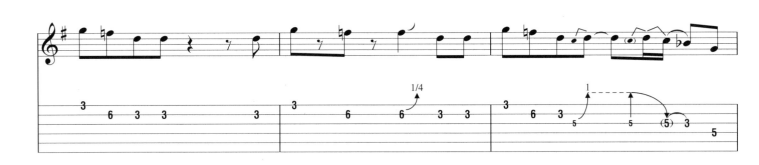

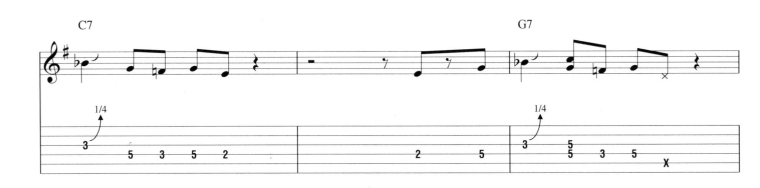

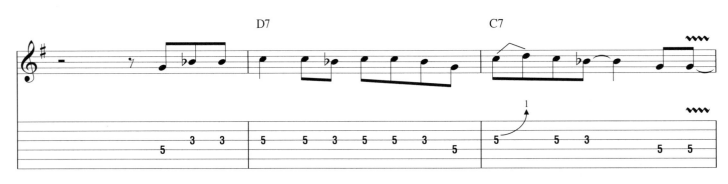

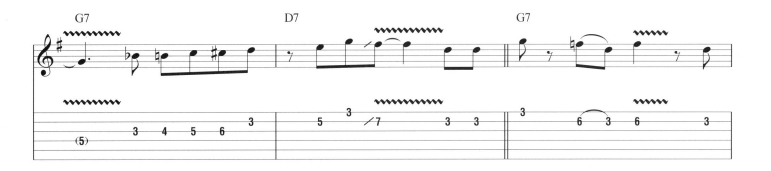

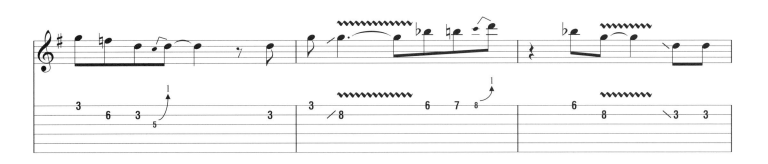

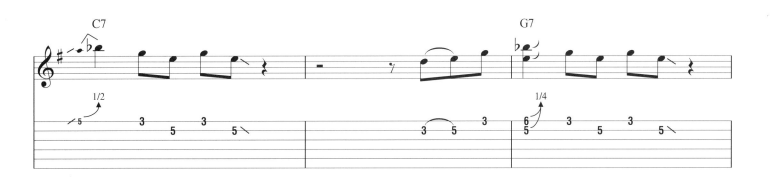

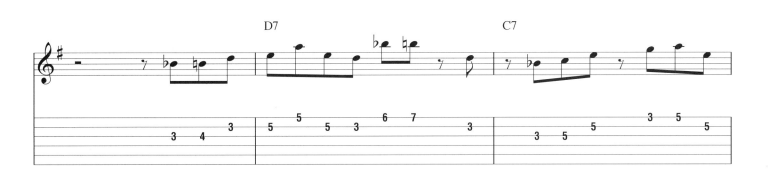

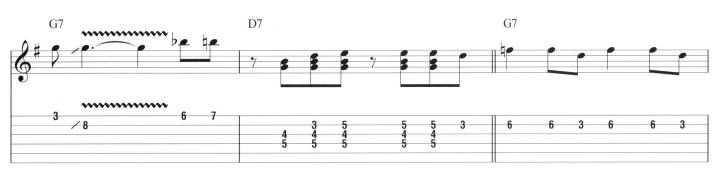

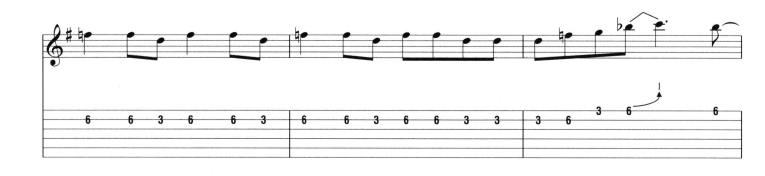

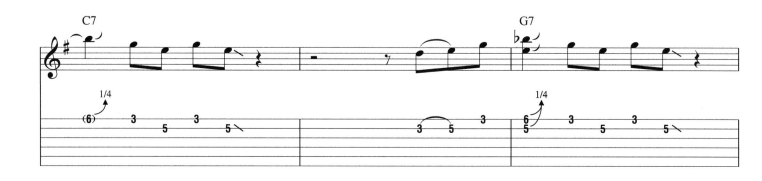

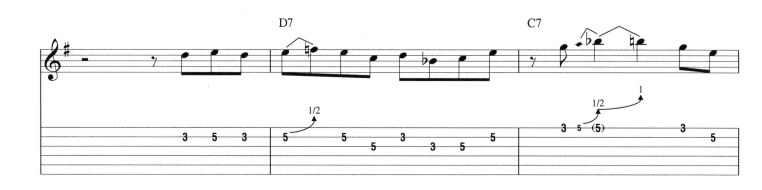

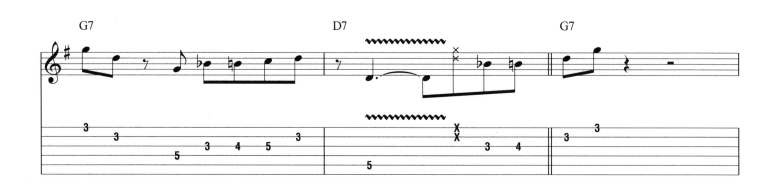

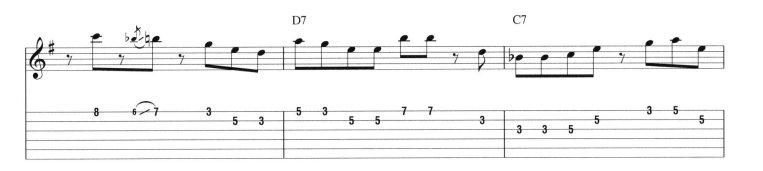

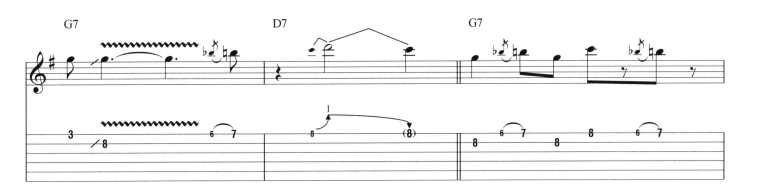

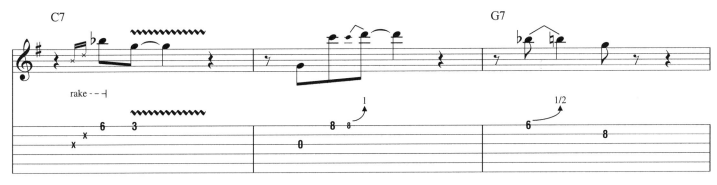

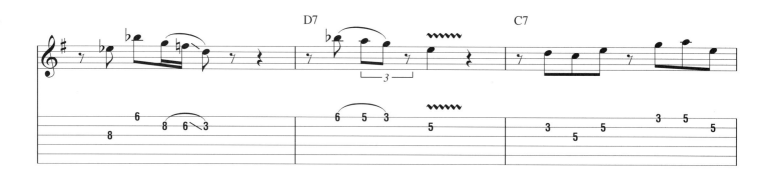

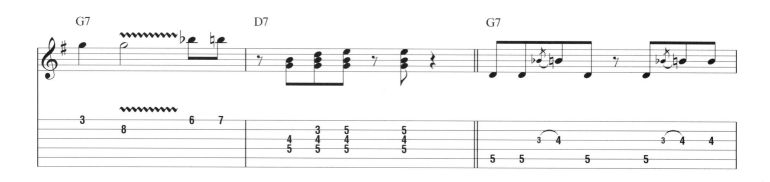

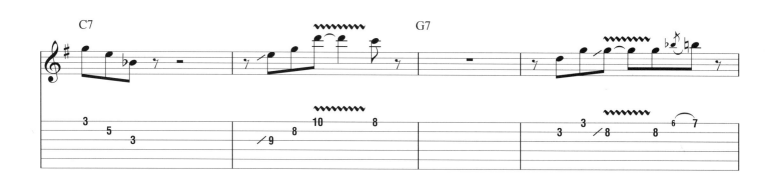

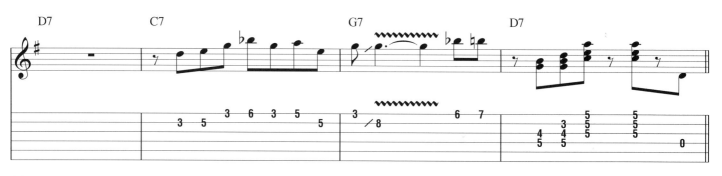

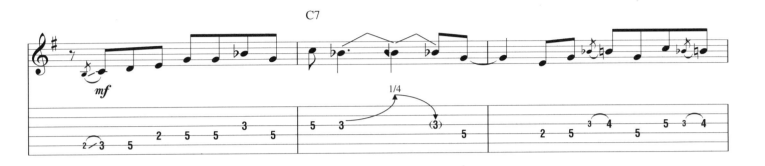

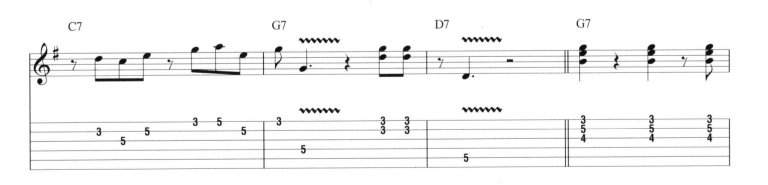

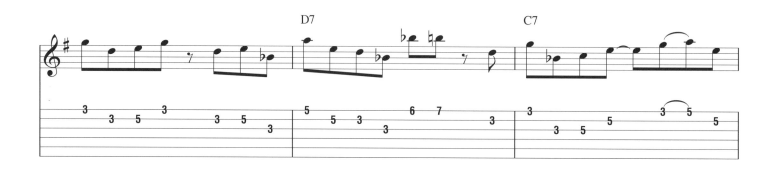

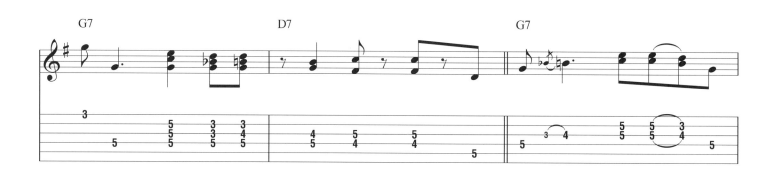

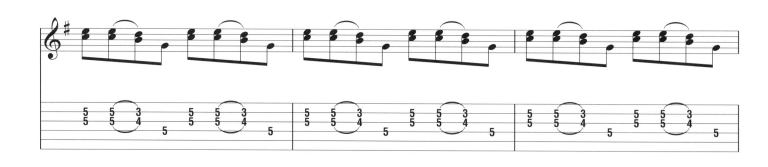

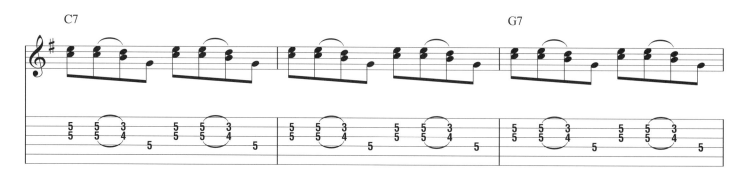

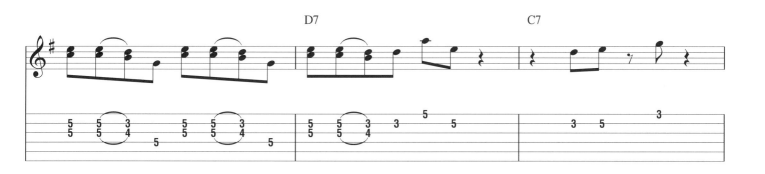

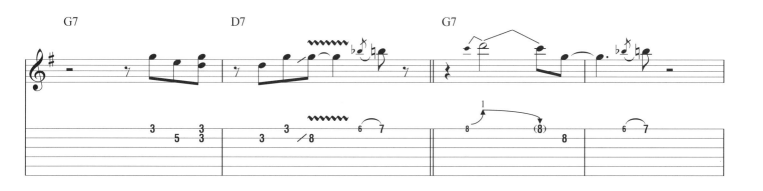

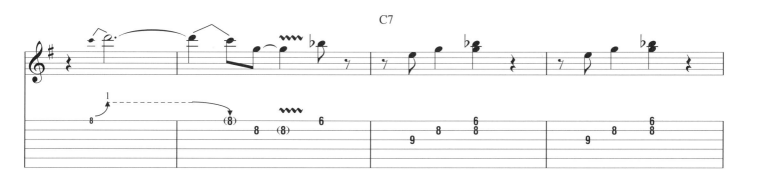

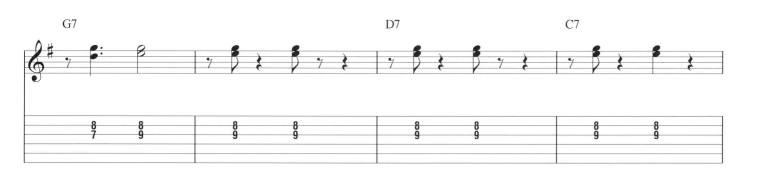

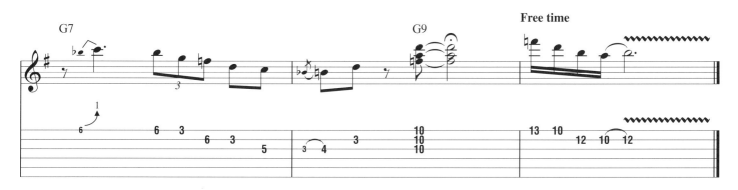

Honky Tonk
(Parts 1 & 2)

**Words and Music by Berisford "Shep" Shepherd,
Clifford Scott, Bill Doggett and Billy Butler**

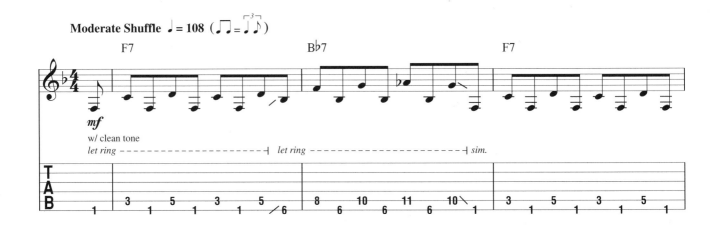

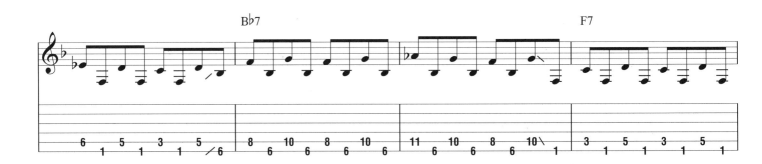

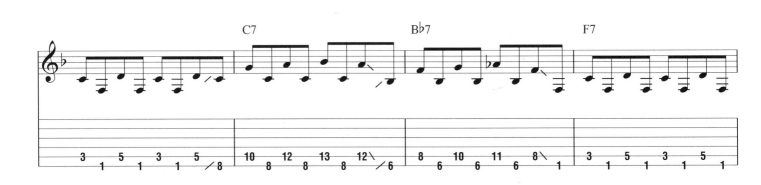

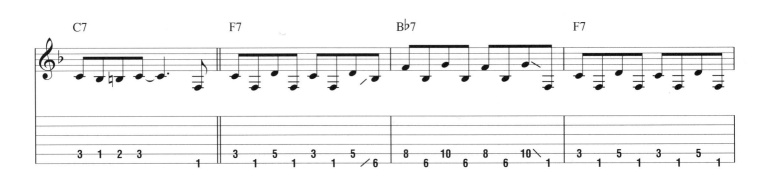

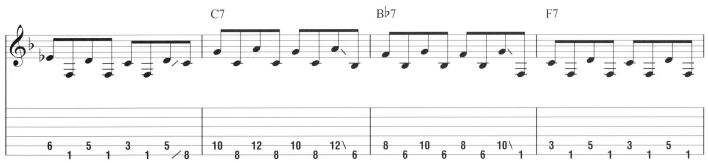

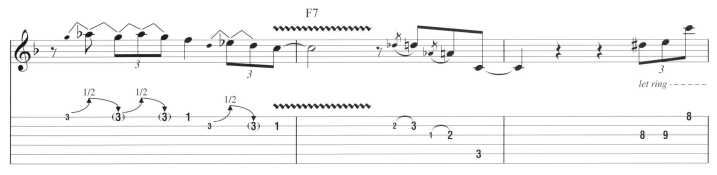

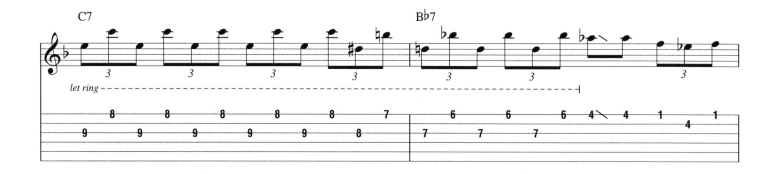

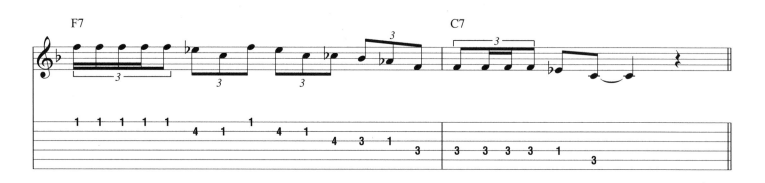

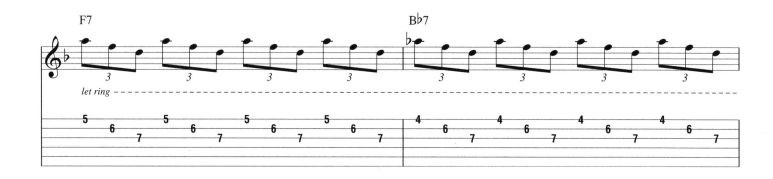

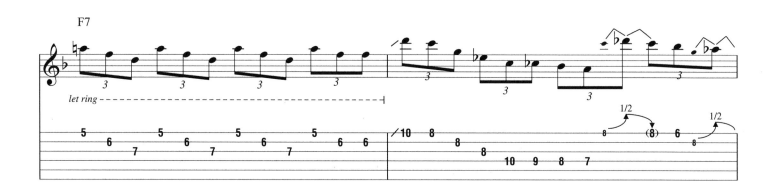

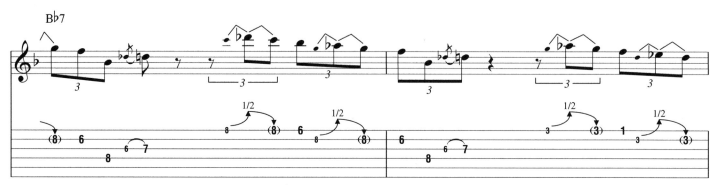

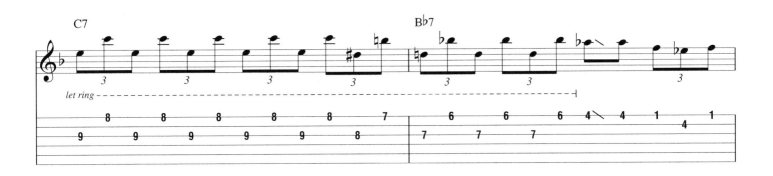

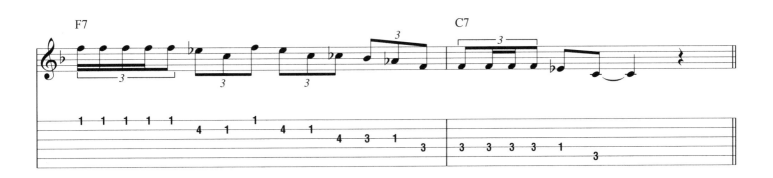

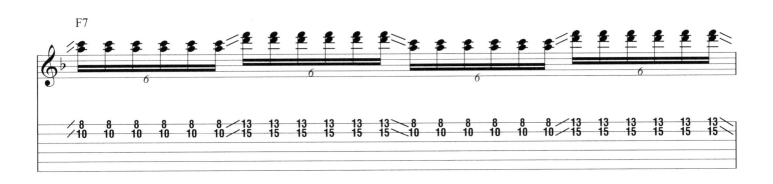

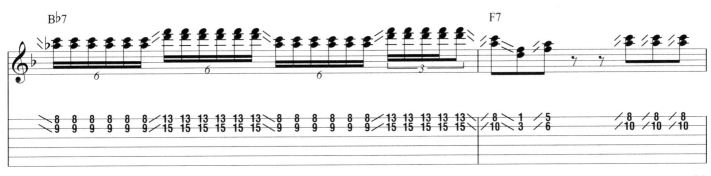

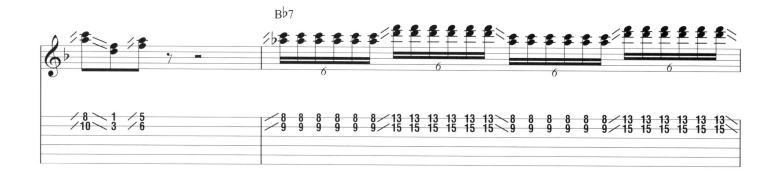

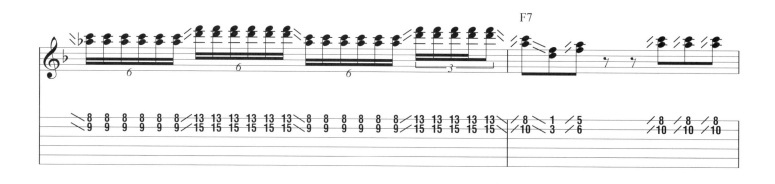

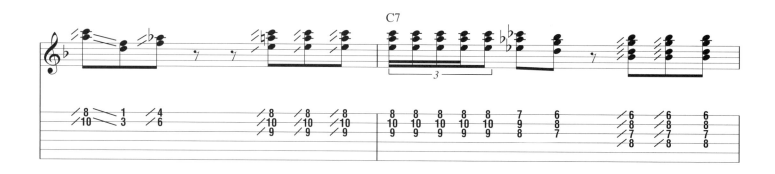

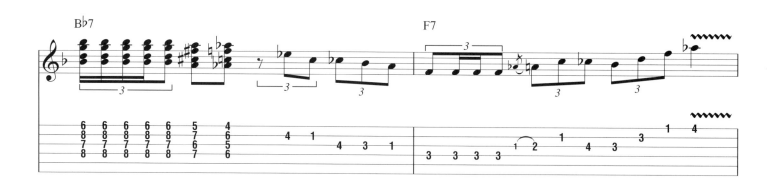

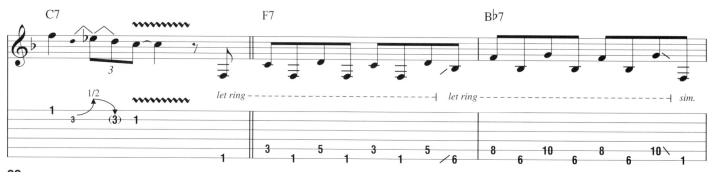

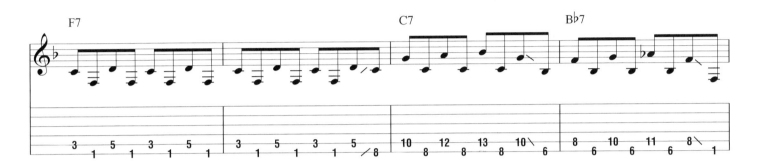

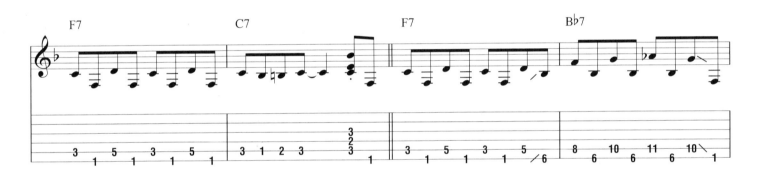

Begin fade

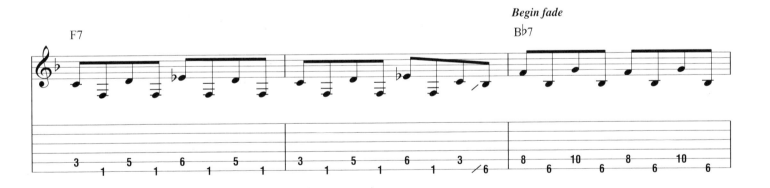

Fade out

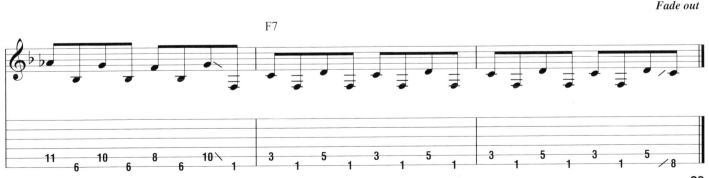

Okie Dokie Stomp

Words and Music by Plummer "Ivory" Davis

Capo XI

Fast Blues ♩ = 182

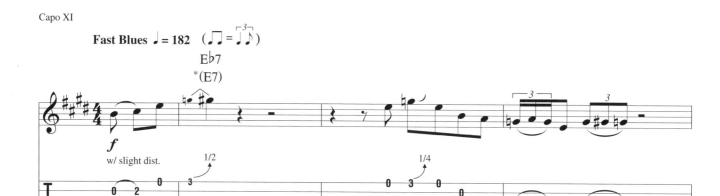

* Symbols in parentheses represent chord names respective to capoed gtr. Symbols above represent actual sounding chords. Capoed fret is "0" in tab.

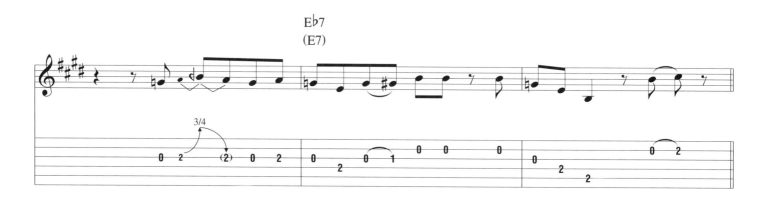

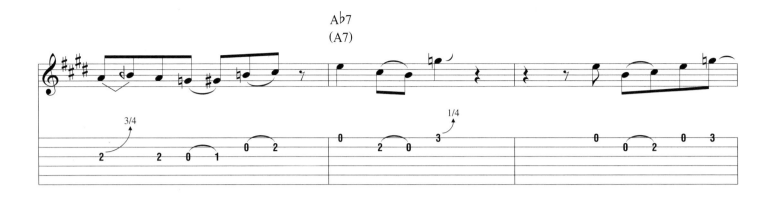

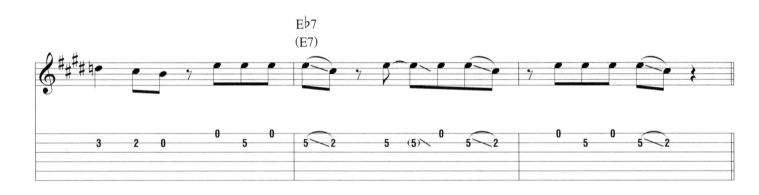

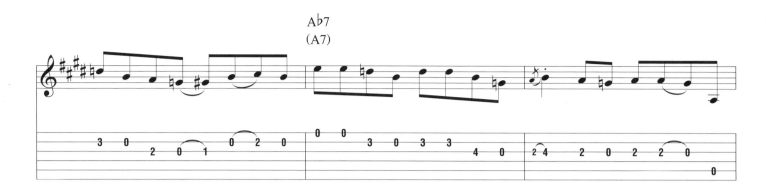

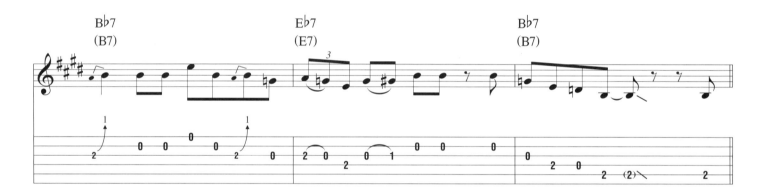

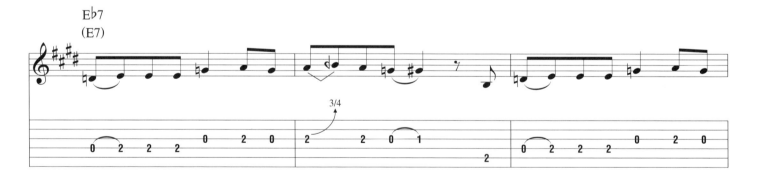

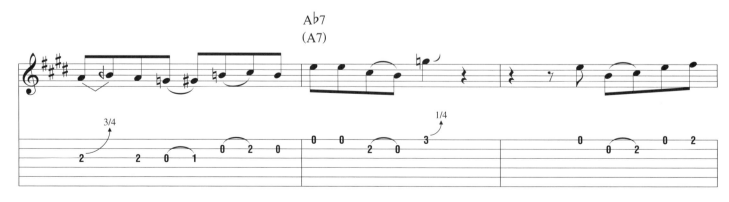

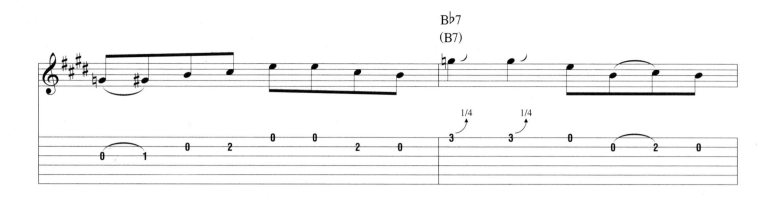

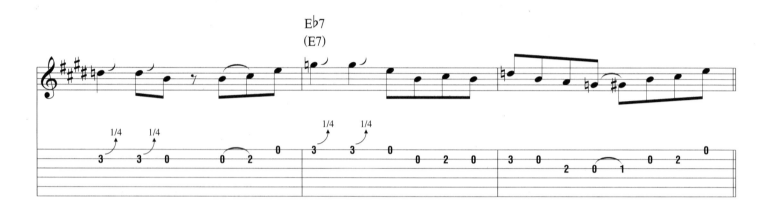

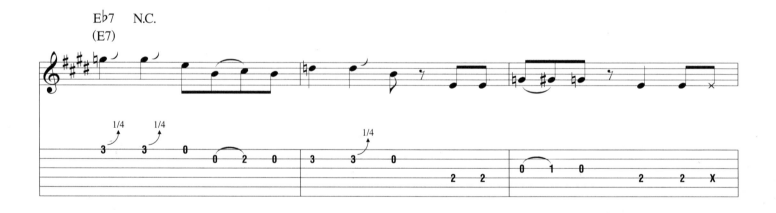

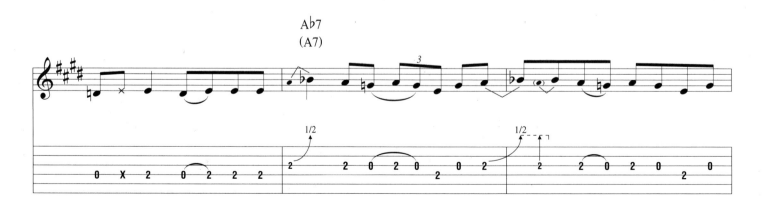

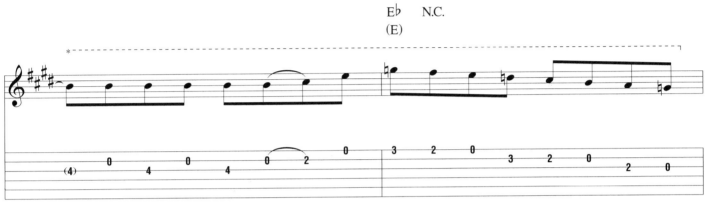

*Played as even eighths.

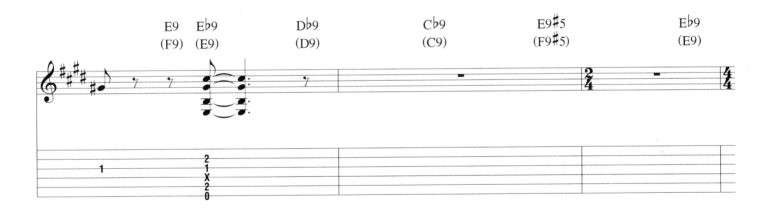

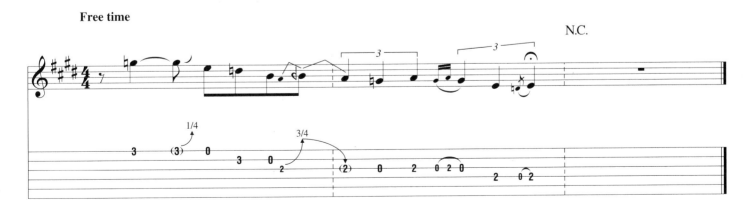

Scuttle Buttin'

Written by Stevie Ray Vaughan

Tune down 1/2 step:
(low to high) Eb-Ab-Db-Gb-Bb-Eb

Moderately fast ♩ = 160

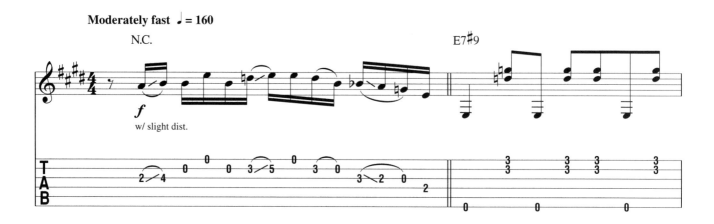

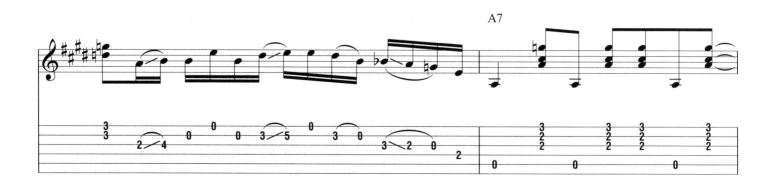

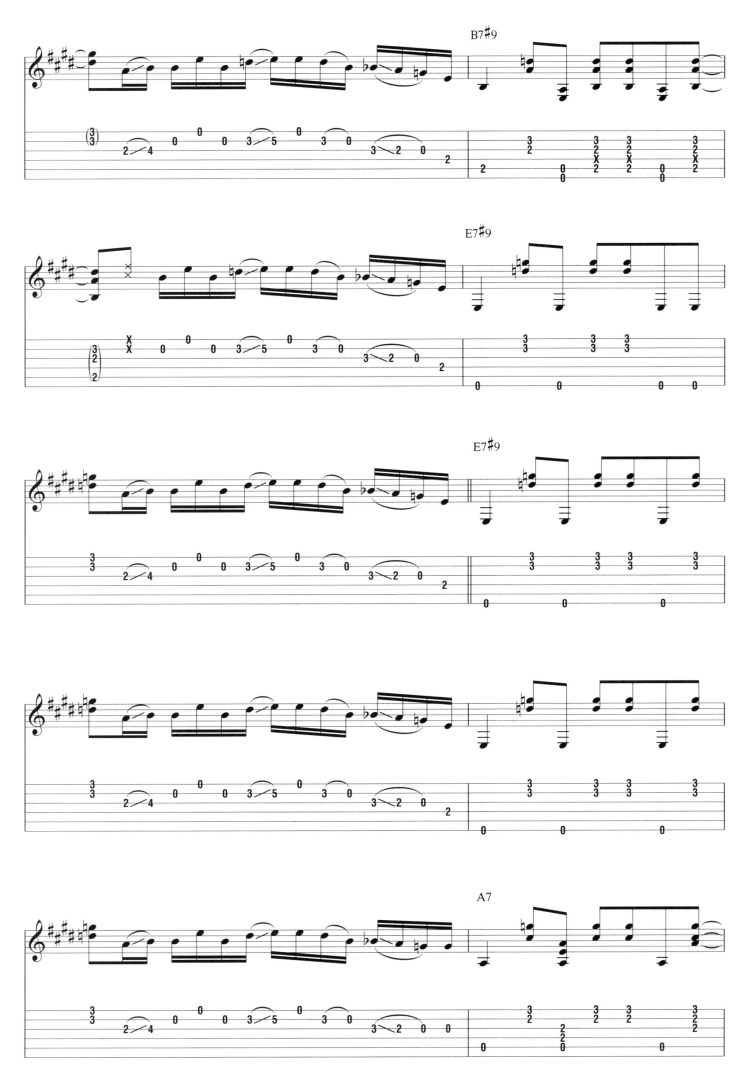

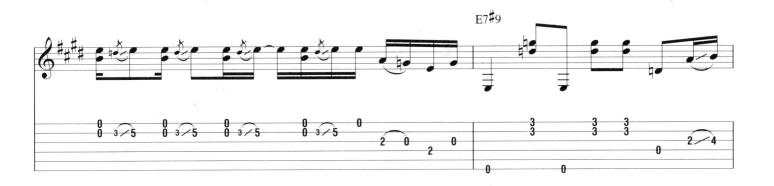

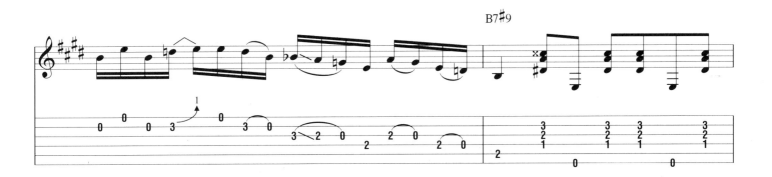

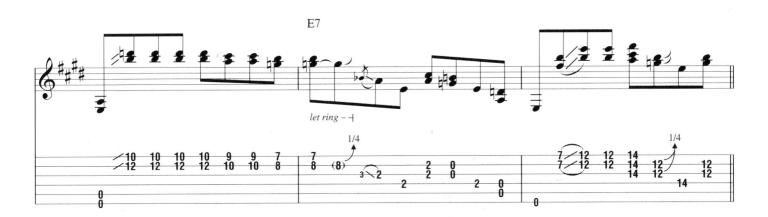

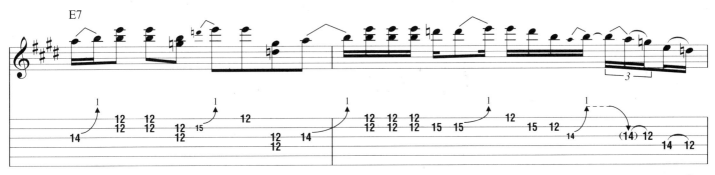

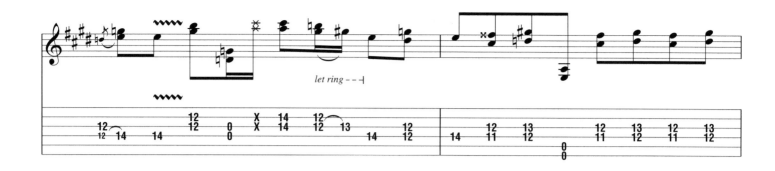

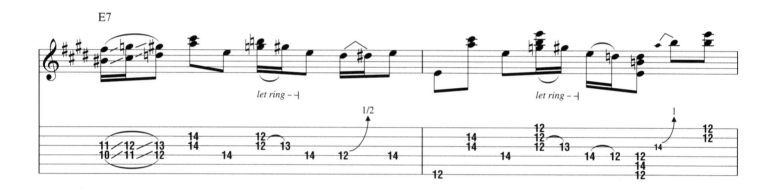

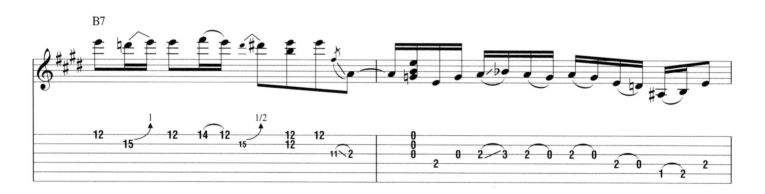

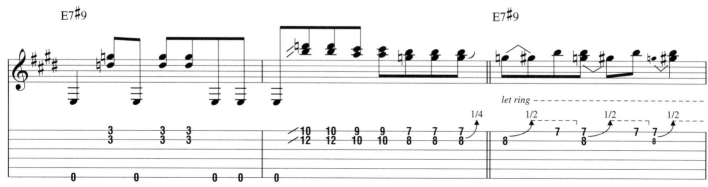

A7

Em7

B7#9

E7#9   N.C.

Steppin' Out

Words and Music by James Bracken

Intro
Fast Blues Rock ♩ = 187

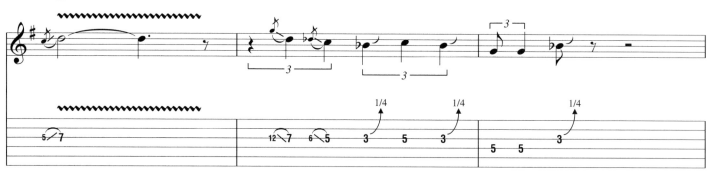

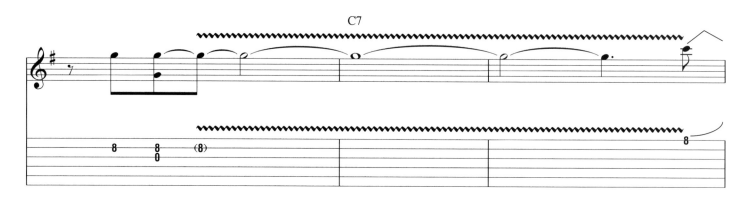

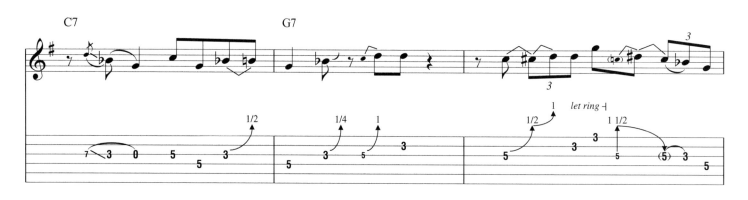

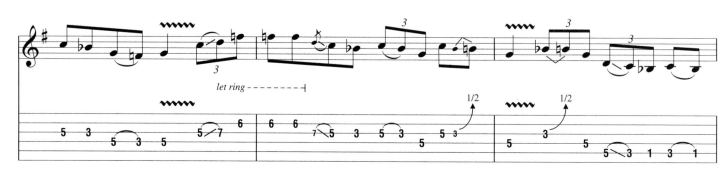

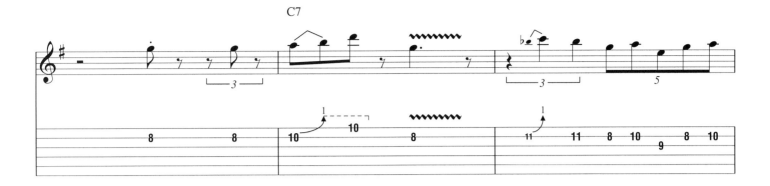

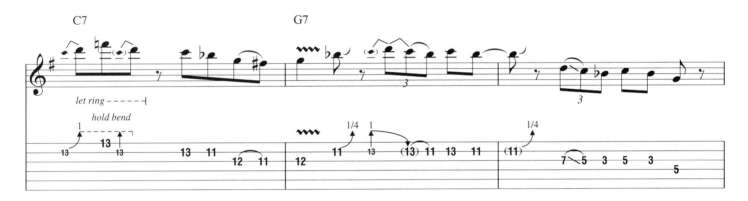

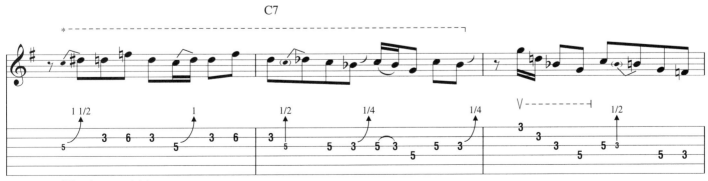

*Played as even eighth notes.

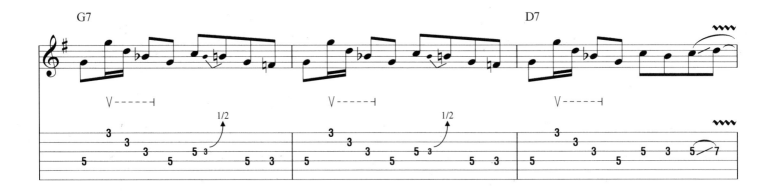

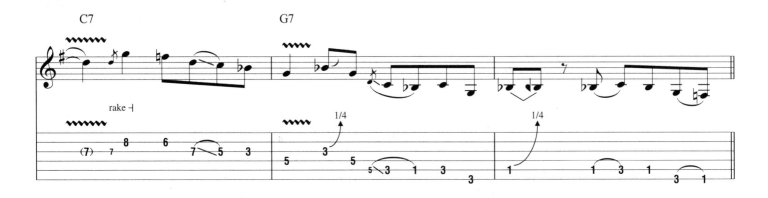

Organ Solo

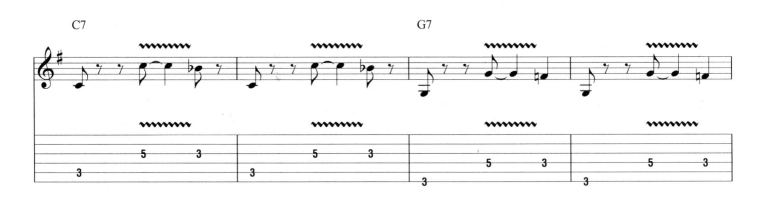

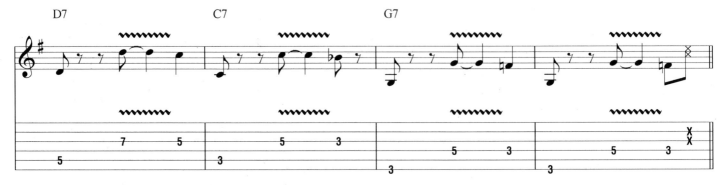

Guitar Solo

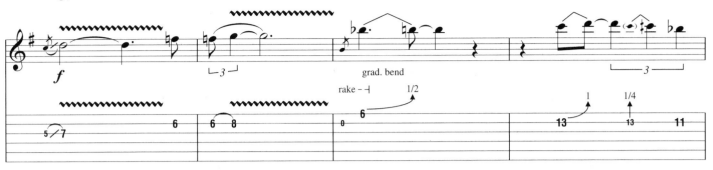

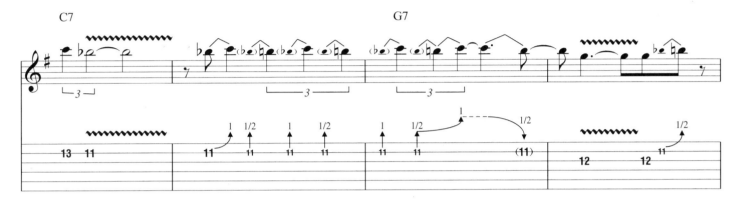

* Played as even eighth
notes.

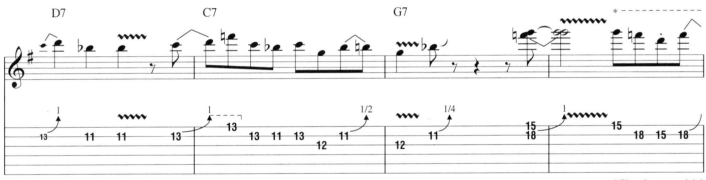

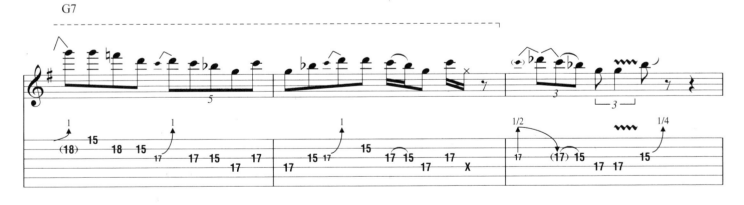

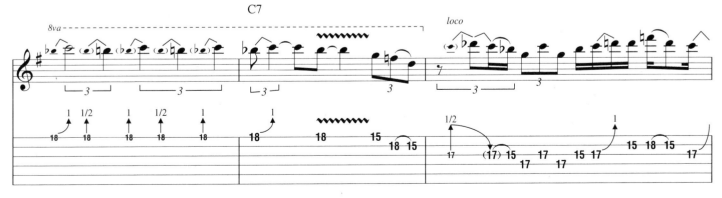

43

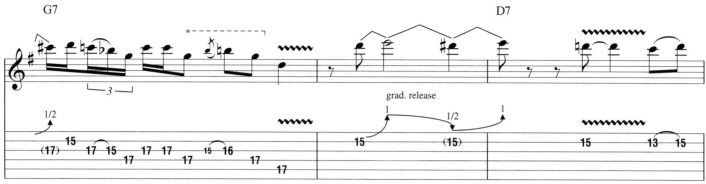

* Played as even eighth notes.

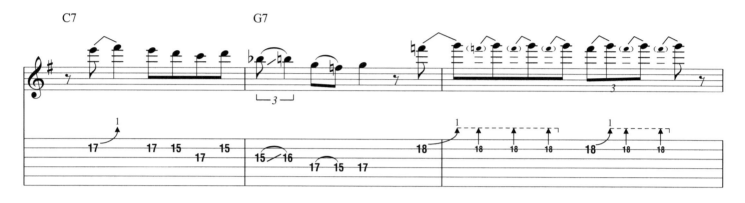

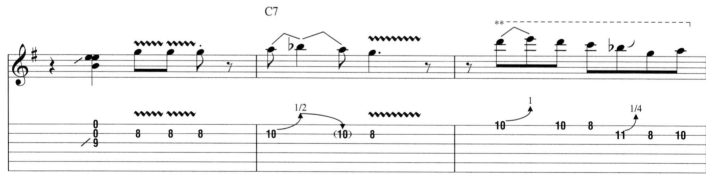

** Played as even eighth notes.

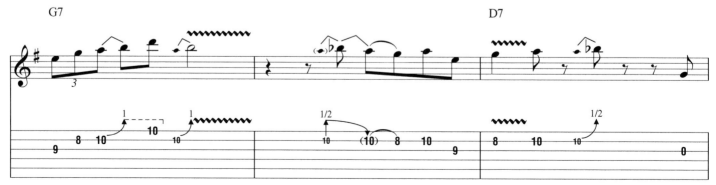

44

Outro

The Stumble

By Freddie King and Sonny Thompson

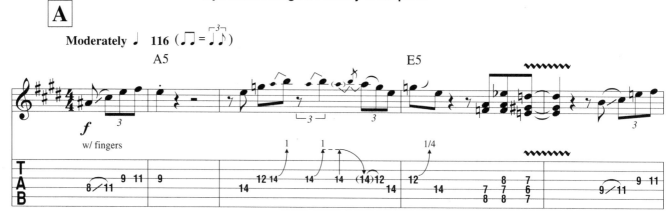

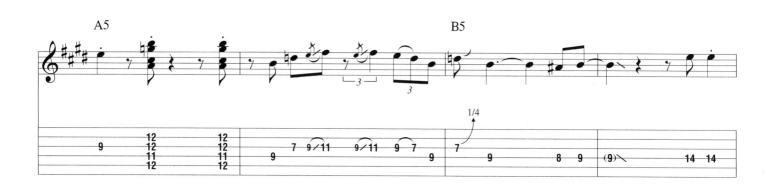

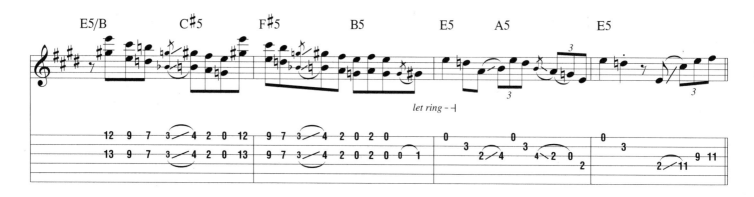

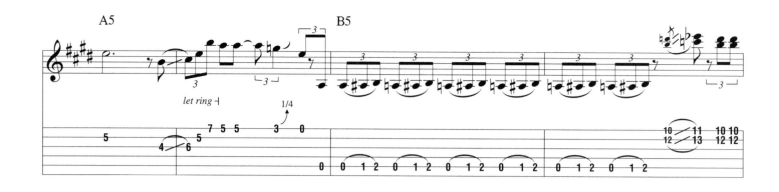

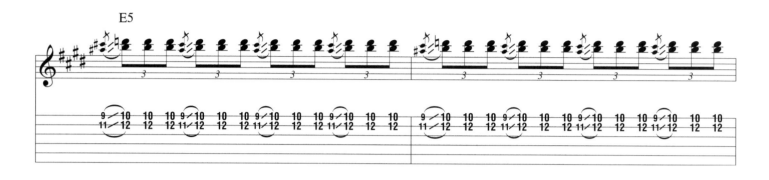

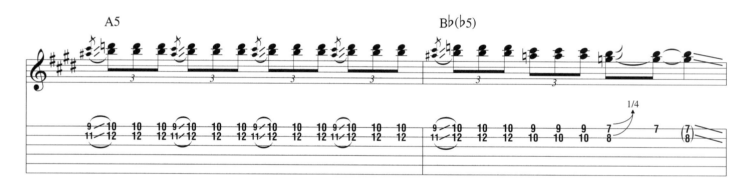

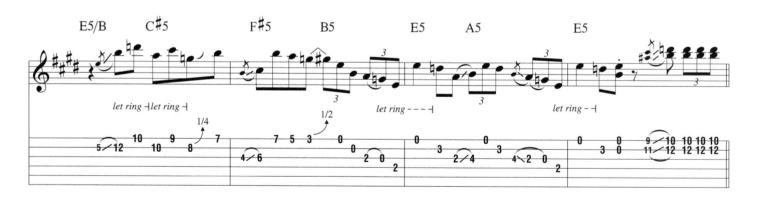

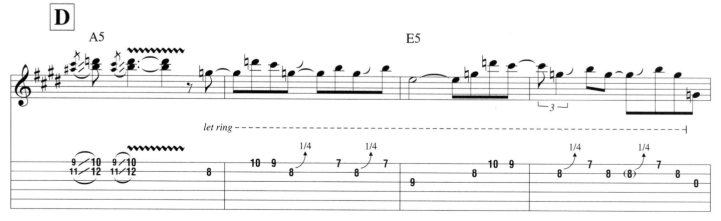

Wham

By Lonnie McIntosh

*Tune down 1 step, Capo III:
(low to high) D-G-C-F-A-D

Fast Blues Rock ♩ = 196

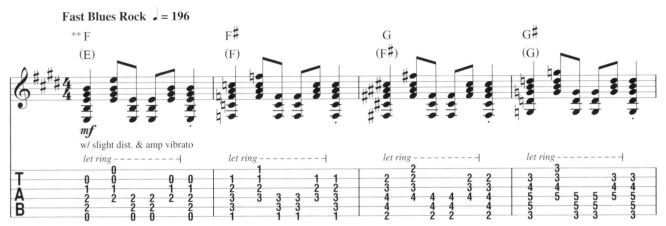

*Song may also be performed by remaining in standard tuning and placing capo at 1st fret.

**Symbols in parentheses represent chord names respective to capoed guitar. Symbols
above represent actual sounding chords. Capoed fret is "0" in TAB.

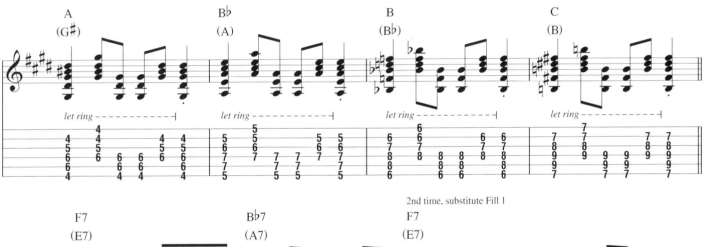

2nd time, substitute Fill 1

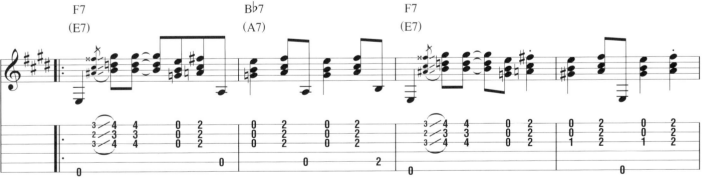

Fill 1

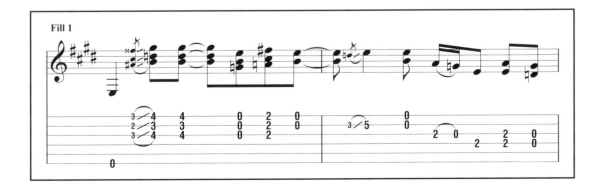

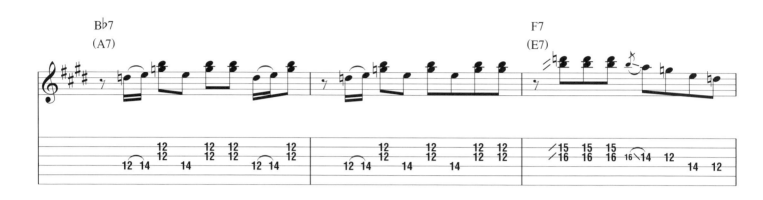

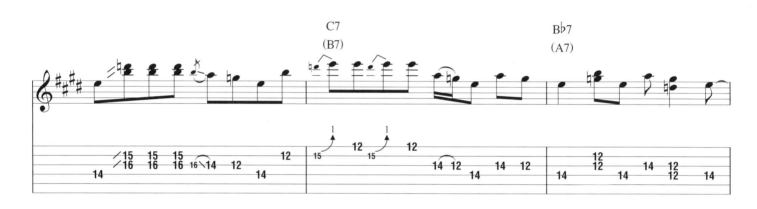

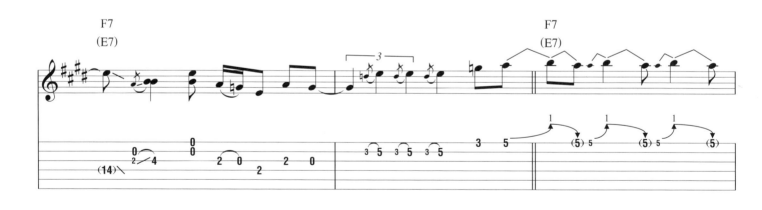

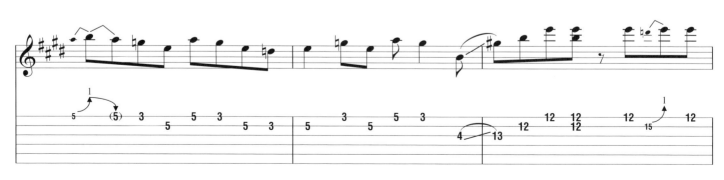

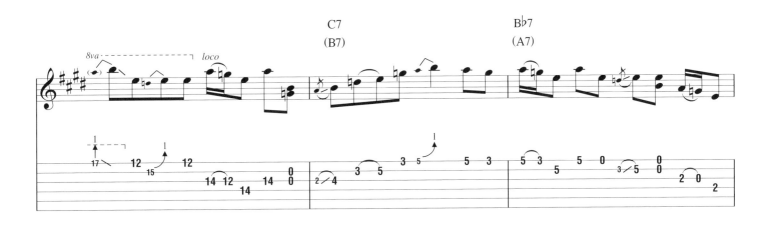

D.C. al Coda   Coda

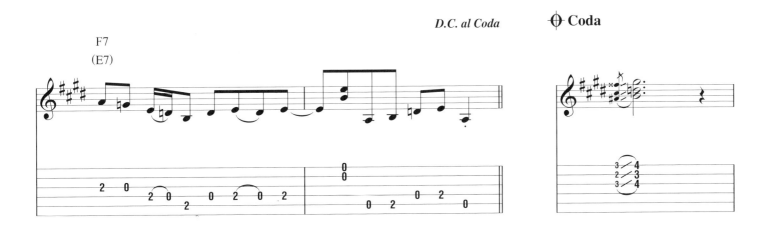

This series will help you play your favorite songs quickly and easily. Just follow the tab and listen to the CD to hear how the guitar should sound, and then play along using the separate backing tracks. Mac or PC users can also slow down the tempo without changing pitch by using the CD in their computer. The melody and lyrics are included in the book so that you can sing or simply follow along.

VOL. 1 – ROCK 00699570 / $16.99
VOL. 2 – ACOUSTIC 00699569 / $16.95
VOL. 3 – HARD ROCK 00699573 / $16.95
VOL. 4 – POP/ROCK 00699571 / $16.99
VOL. 5 – MODERN ROCK 00699574 / $16.99
VOL. 6 – '90s ROCK 00699572 / $16.99
VOL. 7 – BLUES 00699575 / $16.95
VOL. 8 – ROCK 00699585 / $12.95
VOL. 9 – PUNK ROCK 00699576 / $14.95
VOL. 10 – ACOUSTIC 00699586 / $16.95
VOL. 11 – EARLY ROCK 00699579 / $14.95
VOL. 12 – POP/ROCK 00699587 / $14.95
VOL. 13 – FOLK ROCK 00699581 / $14.95
VOL. 14 – BLUES ROCK 00699582 / $16.95
VOL. 15 – R&B 00699583 / $14.95
VOL. 16 – JAZZ 00699584 / $15.95
VOL. 17 – COUNTRY 00699588 / $15.95
VOL. 18 – ACOUSTIC ROCK 00699577 / $15.95
VOL. 19 – SOUL 00699578 / $14.95
VOL. 20 – ROCKABILLY 00699580 / $14.95
VOL. 21 – YULETIDE 00699602 / $14.95
VOL. 22 – CHRISTMAS 00699600 / $15.95
VOL. 23 – SURF 00699635 / $14.95
VOL. 24 – ERIC CLAPTON 00699649 / $16.95
VOL. 25 – LENNON & McCARTNEY 00699642 / $14.95
VOL. 26 – ELVIS PRESLEY 00699643 / $14.95
VOL. 27 – DAVID LEE ROTH 00699645 / $16.95
VOL. 28 – GREG KOCH 00699646 / $14.95
VOL. 29 – BOB SEGER 00699647 / $14.95
VOL. 30 – KISS 00699644 / $14.95
VOL. 31 – CHRISTMAS HITS 00699652 / $14.95
VOL. 32 – THE OFFSPRING 00699653 / $14.95
VOL. 33 – ACOUSTIC CLASSICS 00699656 / $16.95
VOL. 34 – CLASSIC ROCK 00699658 / $16.95
VOL. 35 – HAIR METAL 00699660 / $16.95
VOL. 36 – SOUTHERN ROCK 00699661 / $16.95
VOL. 37 – ACOUSTIC METAL 00699662 / $16.95
VOL. 38 – BLUES 00699663 / $16.95
VOL. 39 – '80s METAL 00699664 / $16.99
VOL. 40 – INCUBUS 00699668 / $17.95
VOL. 41 – ERIC CLAPTON 00699669 / $16.95
VOL. 42 – CHART HITS 00699670 / $16.95

VOL. 43 – LYNYRD SKYNYRD 00699681 / $17.95
VOL. 44 – JAZZ 00699689 / $14.95
VOL. 45 – TV THEMES 00699718 / $14.95
VOL. 46 – MAINSTREAM ROCK 00699722 / $16.95
VOL. 47 – HENDRIX SMASH HITS 00699723 / $19.95
VOL. 48 – AEROSMITH CLASSICS 00699724 / $16.99
VOL. 49 – STEVIE RAY VAUGHAN 00699725 / $16.95
VOL. 50 – NÜ METAL 00699726 / $14.95
VOL. 51 – ALTERNATIVE '90s 00699727 / $12.95
VOL. 52 – FUNK 00699728 / $14.95
VOL. 53 – DISCO 00699729 / $14.99
VOL. 54 – HEAVY METAL 00699730 / $14.95
VOL. 55 – POP METAL 00699731 / $14.95
VOL. 56 – FOO FIGHTERS 00699749 / $14.95
VOL. 57 – SYSTEM OF A DOWN 00699751 / $14.95
VOL. 58 – BLINK-182 00699772 / $14.95
VOL. 59 – GODSMACK 00699773 / $14.95
VOL. 60 – 3 DOORS DOWN 00699774 / $14.95
VOL. 61 – SLIPKNOT 00699775 / $14.95
VOL. 62 – CHRISTMAS CAROLS 00699798 / $12.95
VOL. 63 – CREEDENCE CLEARWATER REVIVAL 00699802 / $16.99
VOL. 64 – THE ULTIMATE OZZY OSBOURNE 00699803 / $16.99
VOL. 65 – THE DOORS 00699806 / $16.99
VOL. 66 – THE ROLLING STONES 00699807 / $16.95
VOL. 67 – BLACK SABBATH 00699808 / $16.99
VOL. 68 – PINK FLOYD – DARK SIDE OF THE MOON 00699809 / $16.99
VOL. 69 – ACOUSTIC FAVORITES 00699810 / $14.95

VOL. 70 – OZZY OSBOURNE 00699805 / $16.99
VOL. 71 – CHRISTIAN ROCK 00699824 / $14.95
VOL. 72 – ACOUSTIC '90S 00699827 / $14.95
VOL. 73 – BLUESY ROCK 00699829 / $16.99
VOL. 74 – PAUL BALOCHE 00699831 / $14.95
VOL. 75 – TOM PETTY 00699882 / $16.99
VOL. 76 – COUNTRY HITS 00699884 / $14.95
VOL. 78 – NIRVANA 00700132 / $14.95
VOL. 80 – ACOUSTIC ANTHOLOGY 00700175 / $19.95
VOL. 81 – ROCK ANTHOLOGY 00700176 / $22.99
VOL. 82 – EASY SONGS 00700177 / $12.99
VOL. 83 – THREE CHORD SONGS 00700178 / $12.99
VOL. 84 – STEELY DAN 00700200 / $16.99
VOL. 86 – BOSTON 00700465 / $16.99
VOL. 87 – ACOUSTIC WOMEN 00700763 / $14.99
VOL. 88 – GRUNGE 00700467 / $16.99
VOL. 96 – THIRD DAY 00700560 / $14.95
VOL. 97 – ROCK BAND 00700703 / $14.99
VOL. 98 – ROCK BAND 00700704 / $14.95
VOL. 99 – ZZ TOP 00700762 / $14.99
VOL. 100 – B.B. KING 00700466 / $14.99
VOL. 103 – SWITCHFOOT 00700773 / $16.99
VOL. 106 – WEEZER 00700958 / $14.99
VOL. 108 – THE WHO 00701053 / $14.99
VOL. 109 – STEVE MILLER 00701054 / $14.99
VOL. 111 – JOHN MELLENCAMP 00701056 / $14.99
VOL. 113 – JIM CROCE 00701058 / $14.99
VOL. 114 – BON JOVI 00701060 / $14.99
VOL. 115 – JOHNNY CASH 00701070 / $14.99
VOL. 116 – THE VENTURES 00701124 / $14.99
VOL. 119 – AC/DC CLASSICS 00701356 / $14.99

Complete song lists available online.

Prices, contents, and availability subject to change without notice.

FOR MORE INFORMATION, SEE YOUR LOCAL MUSIC DEALER,
OR WRITE TO:

HAL•LEONARD® CORPORATION
7777 W. BLUEMOUND RD. P.O. BOX 13819 MILWAUKEE, WI 53213

Visit Hal Leonard online at www.halleonard.com

0110